LABOR'S HISTORIC MISSION

Brian Ellis is Emeritus Professor at La Trobe University, and Professorial Fellow in Philosophy at the University of Melbourne. He published widely in books and articles on philosophy of science, logic and metaphysics, and was the Editor of the Australasian Journal of Philosophy for twelve years. In 1994, Ellis retired from La Trobe, and has since published four more books, including Social Humanism: A New Metaphysics, (Routledge, 2012), which concerns the philosophical foundations of the welfare state. In this essay, Ellis develops a new and more vital philosophy for Labor—one that is consistent with its long and distinguished history.

LABOR'S HISTORIC MISSION

BRIAN ELLIS

PAMPHLETEER

© Brian Ellis 2015

Pamphleteer is an Australian Scholarly imprint.

First published 2015 by Australian Scholarly Publishing Pty Ltd
7 Lt Lothian St Nth, North Melbourne, Vic 3051
TEL: 03 9329 6963 FAX: 03 9329 5452
EMAIL: aspic@ozemail.com.au WEB: scholarly.info

ISBN 978-1-925333-07-7

Contents

Introduction

THE TWO MAIN TRADITIONS OF POLITICAL THOUGHT in Australia have changed their policy profiles considerably since the Second World War. Both have moved to the political right. The Labor Party has rejected the remnants of its nineteenth century socialism, accepted private ownership of most of the means of production, distribution and exchange, made a pact with trade unions to limit wage claims, and evolved into a modern liberally progressive, but socially, and economically conservative, democratic party. The Liberals, on the other hand, have rejected their earlier social liberal agenda, which accepted public ownership of most infrastructure, state universities, and social services. Instead, the Liberal Party has been swept along with the neoliberal tide to become a reactionary conservative party—more like the Tories of Britain and the Republicans in the US, than the Liberals of old. They believe in the corporate state, and, the more radical of them (the free market fundamentalists) seek to remake the whole of society (as far as possible), in the image of a neoclassical perfect market. Consequently, they believe that all of the means of production, distribution, information, and exchange should be firmly in private hands, and that whatever remains in public ownership, other than the police and armed forces, should be sold, or at least corporatised.

This paper is concerned mainly with the Labor tradition, however, and the lessons that are to be drawn from its history and philosophy. Historically, I will argue that Labor's mission has, at least since Federation, been to *work pragmatically* to create a fair, fully employed, and prosperous society. This fact was evident even before Federation. The Frenchman, Albert Metin was so impressed by Australia's social pragmatism, that he published a book entitled 'Socialism without Doctrine' in 1901. Indeed, the pragmatic achievements of state Labor governments were, to his way of thinking, the first indication that a genuinely socialist state could be created democratically, and that Australia was showing the way.[1]

Hugh Collins has identified Australia's unique political stance as Benthamite. '*Political institutions and policies*', he says, '*are to be assessed in terms of the impact of their operation upon the interests of the majority*'. That is, the guiding principle of politics must always be a kind of institutional-cum-legal utilitarianism[2] of the kind that led to the development of the UK People's Charter of 1838. But the Labor Movement in Australia did not evolve from any pre-existing doctrine of natural rights, because the founders of this movement were not natural rights theorists. They were more inclined to believe, as Elie Helévy (1972, p. 138) did, that: 'Governments were instituted, not because man had natural rights, but because he had none.' Therefore, any proposed rights, such as those that might be contained in a worker's charter, would have to be political, not natural, and evaluated as instruments for overall social improvement. Yet, as Collins remarks (pp. 151–2), within ten years of the discovery of gold, practically the whole political program of the Chartists was realised in the Australasian colonies. 'That Chartism should have succeeded so completely in Australia [and New Zealand] by the 1860s, while failing so bitterly in Britain, is doubly significant for any appreciation of Australia's political culture.' (p. 152)

The Second World War was a turning point in the history of many political movements. And the direction of this turning was clearly indicated by the human rights doctrines that emerged at about this time. The most notable of these were President Roosevelt's *Second Bill of Rights* (1944), the *Preamble to the French Constitution for the Fifth Republic* (1946), and the *Universal Declaration of Human Rights* (1948).

These *human* rights doctrines were clearly different in both intention and content from the *natural* rights doctrines of the eighteenth century. The eighteenth century doctrines of *natural* rights were based on medieval theories of *natural* law, which were thought to refer to the inherent rights of humankind. But, in fact, they were proposed as charters for the new republics that their authors were seeking to establish. As such, they were essentially revolutionary documents, and were seen as being so. But the post-war documents were all essentially moral statements, which aimed to bring peace and security to the world. And the rights described were not all thought to be inherent. Therefore, the modern documents were more in the tradition of Chartism than in the eighteenth century one of natural rights. For, they all attempted simply to spell out what ordinary men and women could reasonably ask of their national governments to provide for the good of the people. The *UDHR* argued that states must serve the people, and provide adequately for the dignity, development, and social and economic security of those they are required to serve.

Nevertheless, I will argue, the social democracies and the modern treaties of human rights all have the same theoretical basis. For, any state that was founded on any one of them would have to be a social democracy, or a welfare state of some other kind. It is remarkable, therefore, and a credit to the Dr H. V. Evatt's presidency of the United Nations General Assembly, that this doctrine was passed *nem con* by the General Assembly. To achieve this result, Dr Evatt is on record as having advised the Australian representative on the drafting committee to be pragmatic, and not get bogged down in political theory.[3] It seems, therefore, that Dr Evatt was not only among the early pioneers of the welfare state, but also one who understood clearly that its development required a pragmatic acknowledgement of its moral purpose.[4]

In reality, Dr Evatt was a twentieth century chartist. And the Articles of the *UDHR* were just the principles that the UN representatives at that time thought were sufficiently compelling morally to be worth fighting for.

A distinctive feature of the *UDHR* is that it requires all nations *to provide, as adequately as they reasonably can,* 'through national effort and international co-operation' for '*the economic, social and cultural rights*' which are required, *if people are to live with dignity in their own societies, and be free to develop their own personalities.* This is what it says in Article 22 of the *UDHR*. The economic, social, and cultural rights of mankind, which are all things Mr Hockey would now call 'entitlements', are spelled out in detail in Articles 23 to 29.

The welfare state that evolved in Australia from 1945 to 1975 was extraordinarily successful, as indeed were welfare states everywhere they existed. In France this period is known as 'Les Trentes Glorieuses'. But here it has no name, mainly, I suspect, because Australian socialists were much too doctrinaire to acknowledge these pragmatic achievements. They all wanted much more radical changes to the system of the kinds that Marx and Lenin had argued for. But the welfare state was not the creation of socialist intellectuals; it evolved simply from the intuitive fairness and moral convictions of working people. Yet, it proved to be a very successful kind of state. Throughout the period from 1945 to 1975, GDP per capita rose steadily in Australia (at around 5% per annum, despite the rapid increase in population due to a vigorous immigration policy. And wages/per hour kept in lock-step with productivity. Moreover, the increases in wages and salaries that did occur did so fairly uniformly across all of the quintiles of wage and salary earners, as indeed they did elsewhere in the post-war world. Yet unemployment was almost non-existent. In Australia, it averaged just 2% for the whole of this very productive period, i.e. from 1945 to 1975.

However, the welfare state that existed in Australia was not without its faults. It suffered from most of the social ills of other kinds of states at that time. In the 1940s and fifties, it was exclusive of some minorities. It was technically racist, sexist, and protectionist, extravagant in its use of raw materials, utterly dependent upon the United States strategically, and showed no particular concern for our natural environment. It also contributed heavily to polluting the atmosphere with CFCs and CO_2. So, any revival of the welfare state would clearly have to deal with all of these problems, and with any new problems of a social or economic nature that might arise. In short, it would need to be a welfare state for the 21st century.

Like welfare states everywhere, any new welfare state would need to evolve appropriately, in a manner that respects everyone's rights, as these are laid out in the *UDHR*. For, the *UDHR* should now be seen as a foundation document for ALP, and treated as such. The United Nations Covenants and Protocols, which develop, or enlarge upon, the rights of humankind, must likewise be treated with great respect.[5] For, not to do so would, ultimately, be to undermine the basic document from which these covenants and protocols were developed, and so weaken the demands it should make on ALP policies. Of course, there may be good reasons for changing these conventions, and ultimately the policies. But no signatory to these conventions (as we are) should treat these matters lightly, or act unilaterally to do so, unless its hand is forced by some truly exceptional circumstances. Therefore, if the current ALP is of the view that such circumstances now exist in our region, it is imperative that it should seek to reach accord with all of the nations likely to be affected adversely by these circumstances, act on the agreement reached, and seek the endorsement of the UNHCR on the course of action that we have taken.

Nevertheless, I believe that taking the requisite steps towards creating a welfare state for the 21st century is precisely the task that should be undertaken by the next Labor government. It accords with the history of the Labor movement in Australia to do so, and is a fitting expression of Labor's principal concerns over the years. Plausibly, it is also Labor's historic mission.

1

The Neoliberal Era

THE PERIOD THAT BEGAN WITH THE ELECTIONS OF MARGARET THATCHER IN THE UK AND RONALD REAGAN IN THE US, and ended abruptly with the Global Financial Crisis of 2008, is known as 'the neoliberal era'. Under their leadership, the UK and the US both embraced the political economic theory that is now known as neoliberalism. These policies were initially proposed to deal with the phenomenon of stagflation, i.e. of high rates of inflation occurring in stagnant economies. Stagflation could not be handled easily by the usual tools of economic management, because the measures required would have both to stimulate the economy and curb inflation. The problem was, apparently, that the trade unions would not be willing to reduce their wage demands unilaterally to halt the upwards pressure on costs, and therefore on prices. They argued, reasonably enough, that the inflationary spiral was due to the Oil Crisis, not their wage demands. The conservative governments of the UK and the US tackled the unions head on, blaming their wage demands and feather bedding for the high rates of inflation. But the Australian Labor Government of Bob Hawke sought to work with the unions to negotiate a way out of the problem. And, soon after coming to office, Hawke reached an historic agreement, (known as the Prices and Incomes Accord) with the ACTU to limit wage demands, in exchange for improved social wages (involving increased spending on education and social welfare), and a pledge to minimise inflation.

But, otherwise, the Hawke/Keating Government went along with the 'economic reforms' that Treasury officials were urging. These policies of economic reform were not thought to be challenging, rather than threatening to the ALP. Their greatest problem, they thought, would be to reach a satisfactory accord with the unions.[6] Indeed, throughout the whole period of the Accord process, these reforms appeared to be working well. Australian manufacturing became much more productive and disciplined. Yet, hourly wage rates did not blow out, or stagnate; they remained coupled to productivity, just as they had done throughout the welfare state era. Thus, the profound socio-economic changes, which had been won in Thatcher's Britain only at the cost of great and damaging Trade Union confrontation, were won here without much of a struggle at all. There were boom conditions in the mid to late eighties, resulting in a bust, which resulted in a serious recession in 1990-91, with high unemployment. Nevertheless, the ALP, under Paul Keating's leadership, was credited with having made the transition from a welfare state economy to a modern, and more productive, one without causing working people to suffer unnecessarily. Consequently, although the ALP never regained the popularity that it had achieved in the early years of the Hawke/Keating Government, it retained enough momentum to win the 1994 election.

However, the reformers in Treasury and the Coalition parties had much more in mind than just dealing with the problem of stagflation. Financial deregulation made credit much more readily available, and new technologies radically transformed communications, travel, transport, and access to information. These new technologies were not the result of the reform process. But their appearance at this time certainly made the economic reforms seem much more acceptable. They also provided the reformers with a coherent narrative for more so-called 'economic reform'; one which could be pursued more or less indefinitely. And most conservatives came to see this as a boon. For, if carried to their logical conclusions, the reforms they could demand now in the name of economic progress would prove to be destructive of all of the positive roles that left-leaning governments had always thought were needed to deal with social inequities.

In retrospect, we can say that the economic reforms of the 1980s were, over time, to become a full-scale assault on the agendas of all social democratic governments. They not only undermined the Soviet style 'people's republics' of Eastern Europe and the Soviet Union, which, of course, few people in Australia were worried about. They also undermined all of the welfare states that had flourished in the West in the post-war boom. For, the logical conclusion of the proposed economic reform package was the wholesale destruction of all government social welfare programs (which was manifestly not what Hawke or Keating had in mind).

All good macro-economic theory is based on theories of trade and commerce that were developed initially in the eighteenth century, and refined in the nineteenth. To gain the benefits that the reformers were seeking, many economists argued that *the economy would have to be left alone, so that its invisible hand could do its good work without government interference.* Governments, they said, may legitimately control the overall level of business activity in an economy. But, all redistribution of income or resources, they would say, is necessarily an interference with it. So, bizarre as it may seem, governments do not, from the point of view of pure economic theory, contribute to the economy. They may, in fact, be our largest employers. But, according to the pure theorists, governments are no part of the process of generating wealth. They are, they say, *exogenous.* Their only legitimate roles are therefore meta-economic. Governments can legitimately guarantee that the conditions for the possibility of free trade are maintained, or that legal contracts are honoured. But, as Reagan said in his Inaugural Address in 1981, 'Government is not *the solution* to our problem; government *is* the problem.' And, if this is true of governments, it is also true of all government agencies, and governmentally owned institutions. They must all be parts of the problem.

So, what began in the 1980s as a fairly modest economic reform program was transformed over the years into a radical proposal for restructuring all Western social democracies. *They were to be reconstructed to make them as much like the perfect markets of neoclassical economic theory as possible.* But, if democracy is to survive, such free market fundamentalism must ultimately fail, because its endpoint must involve the business takeover of all of the functions of government, which is roughly what happened a long time ago in the Indian state of Bengal, when its government fell into the hands of the British East India Company. (Lynch, forthcoming)

Thus, the driving force behind neoliberalism was pushing strongly in the direction of some very radical social engineering.

It was not just a proposal for some modest economic reforms for dealing with stagflation. It became, in the hands of extremists, a project to remake the whole of society in the image of the neoclassical economic model—a model that had, in fact, fallen into considerable disrepute due to the Great Depression, which it failed to predict.

There is a great deal of wishful thinking in this radical neoliberal program. No society can be reconstructed as a perfect market, and no market, however perfect, can guarantee that all of its participants will prosper. Inevitably, many will suffer. Real capitalist societies may try to ape perfect markets as best they can. Some neoliberals have even been known to advocate shrinking the roles of government to just defence, and law and order. Governments are *externalities*, they say; so their activities can only be destructive of perfect markets. Nor can perfect markets accommodate social services, or public service organizations, such as parliaments, universities, public hospitals, state schools, or state-owned enterprises. Indeed, from the point of view of a market fundamentalist, just about everything most people really like about our society turns out to be just a side-show.

But today's neoliberal economists are not much fazed by any of this. On the contrary, they are strongly motivated to abolish as many of these institutions as they can, or at least to allow their functions to be taken over by private enterprise. Or, if they cannot sell or abolish them, then, of course, they must at least try to restructure them as business corporations, and require them to act, in so far as they can, in the interests, *not* of the people they were originally meant to serve, but in the interests of the *taxpayers*, whom, ominously, they consider to be the government's only *shareholders*.

The neoliberal era was ushered in during the 1970s. At this time there was a cultural revolution in progress, and people were reacting against the failures of their parents' generation to deal adequately with discrimination against various groups, both nationally and internationally. For the most part, they did not understand, nor did they appreciate, the great social movement that had led to the creation of the welfare states in which they lived, and of which many were beneficiaries.[7] Also, the Cold War was at its height in the 1970s, the Vietnam War was being fought out, and there were riots on the streets and campuses of the USA. And, in this climate, no serious defence of the welfare state against the incursions of free enterprise upon its achievements was possible. It would immediately have been dismissed as Soviet propaganda.

The 1970s was also a period of economic turbulence in the capitalist world, characterised by periods of high inflation and rising unemployment. The causes of these economic developments were never just the trade unions. The major causes appear to have been: (a) the US decision in 1971 to abandon the Bretton Woods agreement, in order to pay for the Vietnam War (by floating the US dollar), and (b) OPEC's decision in 1973 to quadruple the price of crude oil, in order to punish the US and its allies for supporting Israel in the Yom Kippur War.

Plausibly, these events led directly to 'cost-push' inflation and depressed production, and thus to a period of stagflation, which posed serious problems for the kinds of economic management that had, until then, been in vogue. The dominant economic theorists at this time were the monetarists of the Chicago School (led by Milton Friedman), who argued that if you want to stop stagflation, you just have to reduce government expenditure, effectively freeze wages, and reduce taxes on business to stimulate production, i.e. an economic agenda that seemed designed to encourage business enterprises to step up and take control of the national economy.

And, these policies began to be put into effect by governments around the world. Initially, they may have been seen as emergency measures. But the economic advisers of many governments of the day, whose economic theories were mostly neoclassical, had a much more radical agenda. Their aim was nothing less than to remake every capitalist society in the image of a neoclassical perfect market. For, they argued, if the axioms of neoclassical economics were perfectly satisfied, then, the beautiful theorems of neoclassical economic theory must, of logical necessity, all be borne out experimentally. Of course, the same is true of any purely rationalistic theory of economics. It is true, for example, also of Keynesian economic theory. If its axioms are satisfied, then so must its theorems be.

But Keynes's theory does not have such beautiful theorems as the neoclassical one—although, empirically, it is probably a much better theory. Keynes's theory allows dreadful events, such as the great depressions of the 1890s and 1930s, to occur in capitalist economies like ours. Which is true; they did occur. But neoliberal economists did not want use an empirically successful model for society. They preferred the empirically unsuccessful neoclassical model, which had much nicer theorems. So, in order to put an end to depressions and other economic nasties, many economic advisers to governments (and to business corporations, which stood to profit enormously from their advice) opted for the neoclassical form of economic rationalism. They argued, with their hands on their hearts, that: *if a society could be reconstructed*

17

in the image of a perfect neoclassical market, then all of the beautiful theorems of neoclassical economics must in practice be realised. This is the mantra of neoclassical economic rationalism. It requires, among other things, that every function of government that can be privatised should be privatised, and every function that cannot be privatised should, if possible, be corporatized. Governments must, the economic rationalists say, be shrunk as much as possible, so that Adam Smith's invisible hand can be left alone to do its divine work. It is hard to imagine a more blatant, or more irresponsible, abandonment of empirical scientific method.

With the election of Margaret Thatcher in 1979, and Ronald Reagan in 1981, to lead the governments of their respective countries, this very radical, and highly idealised, political agenda began to be put into practice. They privatised everything they could, and the organisations they could not privatise, they reconstructed to make them look as much like corporations as possible. And, the apparent success of their programs in the early days of the revolution led to the entrenchment of their neoliberal philosophy for more than a generation. Business flourished, especially Big Business, and the economists who advised them flourished too. Consequently, money poured into the coffers of neoliberal political parties everywhere.

Yet, as I will argue, this success was more apparent than real, because the neoliberal era has been built on debt, deception, and a radical redistribution of wealth and services all the way up from the poorest of the poor to the richest of the rich. There have been some big rises in productivity, but also huge increases in the levels of private debt. However, the real increases in productivity have, in fact, had very little to do with neoliberalism. They have been due almost entirely to: (a) *technological advances*, especially in computing and the internet, which, of course, occurred in every technologically advanced society in the world, whether neoliberal or not; (b) the liberation of women, which greatly increased the size and power of the educated workforces of all advanced capitalist societies; and (c) the transfer of power, money, and privilege from the poorer sections of society to the richer ones, creating a new category super-rich individuals who are mostly beyond the reach of governmental powers of taxation.

2

The Philosophy of Neoliberalism

THE ECONOMIC REVOLUTION, WHICH THE NEOLIBERAL REVOLU-
TION HAS UNDOUBTEDLY PRODUCED, LIES IN THE AREAS OF FREE
TRADE AND FINANCIAL DEREGULATION. Free trade, in the form of
globalization, appears to have provided enormous benefits to the
developing world. It has raised their levels of prosperity rapidly,
and probably sustainably. And for this achievement it deserves
some credit, even though this result was probably unintended[8].
But financial deregulation has also led to unprecedented increases in the levels of debt in the developed world. Consequently,
the world is once again threatened with the prospect of debt de-
flation, which is, plausibly, the mechanism that led to the Great
Depression. The present generation, which enjoyed spending all
this money, appears to be grateful for the support and encour-
agement it gave to big spenders. But it will almost certainly be
very bad for the future generations, who, presumably, will one
day have to pay for it all.

The neoliberal era has been widely accepted as a time of great prosperity. We no longer live in the technically disconnected world of the seventies. At that time, most information was stored in libraries, cultural icons were stored in museums or art galleries, communications were limited and time-consuming, and social media did not exist. But we have since become a technically very connected world, in which information is now mostly at our fingertips. Almost anything that we might ever want to know, hear, see, or listen to, is accessible on our iPhones or iPads. For, these tiny instruments, which can be purchased for just a few hundred dollars, provide us with ready access to nearly all of the libraries, museums, art galleries, concert halls, cinemas, CDs, and friends or acquaintances that we might ever wish to see, hear or visit. Moreover, these same instruments contain cameras, tour guides, search engines, timetables, and recorders, which, previously, would have been regarded as miraculous. The paradox is that these astounding increases in our capacities to communicate and inform ourselves do not show up as being significant progress anywhere in the published economic data.

Jane Gleeson-White (2014) has explained that this is because our accounting methods are out of date. We now live in a post-industrial world, she says. Yet, we account for *the costs of goods and services*, as though their acquisition were the ends of human endeavour. But we do not account for *what these goods or services enable us to do*. And, what is manifestly true is that the digital revolution has increased human potentialities for action and experience by many orders of magnitude. If our theory of the wealth of nations were a dynamic rather than a static one, which measured wealth not by *what things cost*, but by *what they enable people to do*, then the post-industrial world would be seen immediately to be many times wealthier than the one we left behind.

But few, if any, of these changes are due to the *economic* system that has prevailed in the West for the past thirty years or so. That system, which is reflected in our economic theories, is, in fact, a relic of the nineteenth century. In the nineteenth century, it is true that one's wealth could reasonably be measured by one's stock of capital goods. For these, together with health and level of education, were then the principal determinants of our capacities for action.[9] But, in terms of these classical measures of wealth, we are not much better off now than we were before the digital revolution began. We live in a technically highly interconnected world, in which good health and high levels of education are normal, and, potentially, we are all very much better off than we were before. And, whatever our backgrounds, we can mostly do all sorts of things now that our ancestors could not even imagine doing. And, the new connectedness of people is *almost entirely* due to the digital technology, which was developed during and after the Second World War, and the subsequent design, miniaturization, and manufacture of ingenious machines to exploit it. Neoliberalism has had very little, if anything, to do with it.

The first of these developments in digital technology occurred just as much in the social democracies of Northern Europe and Japan, as it did in the US, UK or British Commonwealth. It is true that much of the continuing research and development, which was required to produce the new instruments of communication, occurred in the US, whose tertiary educational system has undoubtedly led the world since the 1920s. But these instruments were *technological* triumphs, not economic or political ones. And their development was *an international* one, to which Japan, Finland, Germany and many other countries made significant contributions. So, no special credit is due to the neoliberal political philosophy, which came, by chance, to dominate the US, UK and the British Commonwealth just at the time that this technology was beginning to yield such wonderful results.[10]

The liberalizations of finance and trade, which were among the hallmarks of neoliberalism, did have major social consequences. They sparked an explosion of borrowing and spending on world markets on a scale that has never been seen before. In Australia, the level of private debt rose to 160% of GDP in 2008, which is about $1.6 trillion. But the explosion of financial activity did not produce the technological revolution. It produced asset price bubbles, and unprecedented levels of debt. The closest parallels in Australia to these events were the boom times that preceded the great depressions of the 1890s and 1930s, when unregulated borrowing and spending were the order of the day. Consequently, when the GFC occurred in 2008, many people thought that the Great Recession might turn into yet another Great Depression. It still might. Much of the world is still heavily debt-ridden, and might yet suffer the long and painful process of 'debt deflation', which is thought to be the mechanism that created and sustained the Great Depression (Irving Fisher, Hyman Minsky). The present generation, which enjoyed spending all this money, appears to be grateful for the support and encouragement neoliberal governments gave them. But it will almost certainly be very bad for the future generations, who will eventually have to pay it all back.

The first decade of the neoliberal era was a time of social turmoil in Britain, and also one of wild speculation on stock exchanges and financial markets around the world. There was an unexplained boom in stock prices in 1987, which led to a deep recession in market economies everywhere in the early nineties. Consequently, it could be argued that our exchange rates, GDPs, unemployment figures, and other economic variables of the eighties and early nineties are not reliable indicators of the economic success or otherwise of neoliberal political philosophy. But, since 1992, it is fair to say that the economies of the neoliberal states have all begun to stabilize somewhat, and show their true worth.

The figures for Australia show that after some fluctuations in the eighties, leading up to the 'recession we had to have', unemployment declined from its recession high of 10.9% in 1992 to a low of 4.1% in 2008. Our current account deficit, on the other hand, increased in fits and starts from near zero in 1980 to about 5 billion per quarter in 1990. It remained at about that figure for a decade or so. And then, in 2002, it *began a steep decline, and plunged down to about* $20 billion *per quarter by* 2008, which was at the end of Mr. Howard's term of office. Thereafter, it has oscillated wildly between quarterly deficits of $5 billion and $20 billion per quarter. That is, our current account deficit has been accumulating at approximately $7.5 billion per quarter on average for 30 years, i.e. by $900 billion for the whole period (since current account deficits are necessarily cumulative). Moreover it showed no sign whatever of tapering off before the GFC of 2008. On the contrary, the current account deficit for the final quarter of 2008 was about $20 billion.

Real GDP growth in the neoliberal era has, on the other hand, been rather sluggish. And, this is so, despite the fact that the neoliberal policy of mortgaging Australia has pumped nearly a trillion dollars into the economy over the thirty-year period from 1980 to 2008. If I were a young person today, I should be very, very angry. Our wealth as a nation has manifestly been squandered, and there is almost nothing to show for it. Real GDP growth has remained at well below the levels achieved regularly in the years of Australia's welfare state. It has not—not even once—reached the levels achieved regularly in the welfare state era. The *highest* rate of real GDP growth in the neoliberal era was 4.7% in 2000. But, according to Steven Bell (1997), the *average* growth rate from 1960 to 1974 was 5.2%.

3

The Problem of Unemployment

GIVEN THESE FIGURES, IT SEEMS THAT AUSTRALIA HAS CHRON-
IC PROBLEMS WITH BOTH UNEMPLOYMENT AND DEBT. These two
problems are linked, and both were undoubtedly creations of
the neoliberal era. They are linked, because the two problems
were created by the policy of deregulation, and consequently the
neglect of social objectives and long-term aims. So, I believe, we
must begin the process of re-regulation, with a view to creating
the kind of society we want for our children and grandchildren.
Fortunately, we have glimpsed this possible future in our own
past. The post-war welfare state certainly had its faults. But they
were all social faults, which were *the detritus of our deep past*,
not the products of our new beginnings after the war. Racism,
sexism, blatant protectionism, environmental neglect, animal
cruelty, and the social exclusion of minorities were all among our
socially inherited traits. But they were all world-wide phenomena
at that time, and every civilized country in the world has had a
past like this, and was prone to such socially divisive attitudes in

the early post-war years.

Nor is the threat of anthropogenic climate change one that can be laid at the feet of the welfare state. It is a serious problem, which requires urgent action. But prosperous nations everywhere, and of every political color, contributed to its creation, and none is uniquely fitted to deal with it. Naomi Kline (2014) has argued that the selfishness of capitalism got us into this mess, and has systematically been blocking moves to cope with it. No doubt it has. But my case for the developing a new kind of welfare state does not depend upon this thesis. All of the technologically advanced countries in the world have been responsible for the atmospheric changes that have caused the problem. And, they might have occurred anyway, even if they had all been social democracies. Capitalism has been responsible for getting us almost irretrievably into debt, and making any solution to the problem much more difficult to achieve. All I need to say now is that that the solution to the problem is one that will require planning and social coordination, and that welfare states have shown themselves to be willing to take such action.

So, what must be done seems obvious. We must work towards the creation of a welfare state that is without any of the faults that might retrospectively be attributed to earlier versions; *we must aim to create a new kind of welfare state for the 21st century.* This is what is clearly required. It is also, I think, Labor's historic mission.

4

The Post-war Movement

In 1945, Ben Chifley became Prime Minister of Australia, and set out to create what he called a 'new golden age of peace and shared prosperity' in Australia. Australia was not the only country to have such ambitions. All of the countries that are now classified as social democracies (and some that have since turned the clock back to the pre-Depression era) shared this ambition. Chifley was inspired by his own deep concerns for people's welfare, and believed that the task of government is to create a prosperous nation in which ordinary people can live well, and develop their own personalities. He was a centralist, but not an autocrat. He was a firm believer in democracy and democratic processes. That is, he was a social democrat. Dr. Evatt was Chifley's Deputy Prime Minister, Attorney General, and Minister for External Affairs. In 1948, he was elected as the third President of the General Assembly of the United Nations. And, under his stewardship, the General Assembly passed the *Universal Declaration of Human Rights* without dissent.

The *Universal Declaration* was only one of a number of humanistic documents concerned with human rights written at about this time. Franklin D Roosevelt announced a Second Bill of Rights in his State of the Union Address of January 1944. Roosevelt, who died about a year later, made his announcement specifically in response to the horrors of the Great Depression. At the conclusion of his address, Roosevelt called for the newsreel cameras to make this historic statement:

… In our day these economic truths have become accepted as self-evident. We have accepted, so to speak, a second Bill of Rights under which a new basis of security and prosperity can be established for all regardless of station, race, or creed. Among these are:

- The right to a useful and remunerative job in the industries or shops or farms or mines of the Nation;
- The right to earn enough to provide adequate food and clothing and recreation;
- The right of every farmer to raise and sell his products at a return which will give him and his family a decent living;
- The right of every businessman, large and small, to trade in an atmosphere of freedom from unfair competition and domination by monopolies at home or abroad;
- The right of every family to a decent home;
- The right to adequate medical care and the opportunity to achieve and enjoy good health;

- The right to adequate protection from the economic fears of old age, sickness, accident, and unemployment;
- The right to a good education.

All of these rights spell security. And after this war is won we must be prepared to move forward, in the implementation of these rights, to new goals of human happiness and well-being. America's own rightful place in the world depends in large part upon how fully these and similar rights have been carried into practice for our citizens. For unless there is security here at home there cannot be lasting peace in the world.

The Constitution of the Fifth Republic of France was a third such document. It prescribed, among other things, that women should have equal rights with men in all spheres, that any person persecuted in virtue of his or her actions in favour of liberty may claim asylum upon any of the territories of the Republic, and that everyone has a duty to work, as well as a right to employment. Like the other two documents, this one required the government of the day to act positively to provide for human rights, not just negatively to prevent interference with them.

5

Human Rights *versus* Natural Rights

THESE POST-WAR DOCTRINES WERE WRITTEN FOR IMPORTANTLY
DIFFERENT REASONS FROM THEIR EIGHTEENTH CENTURY COUN-
TERPARTS. The eighteenth century authors were all familiar with
the early Renaissance conception of Natural Law. Accordingly,
they set out to define what they called the *natural rights* of mankind. These were the supposedly inalienable moral rights that we
are somehow naturally endowed with (whether by nature or by
God is unspecified). But the conception of a *human* right, which
is implicit in all the modern doctrines, is more of the nature of a
guarantee (e.g. by a government, or by the authority of the United Nations) than a statement of any pre-existing natural right.
Roosevelt spoke of a second bill of rights, explicitly acknowl-
edging their legal status. The authors of the Constitution of the
Fifth Republic of France specifically recognised the rights they
described in the Preamble as *obligations of the state*.

Secondly, the eighteenth century doctrines were all written
with the aim of defining the limits of government power in the

new republics they were hoping to create. They did not wish to depose the king, only for him to be replaced by some other kind of despot. Their common aim was to restrict the kinds of laws that could be enacted in the kinds of republics they were hoping to build. And these doctrines were all essentially revolutionary documents. The slogan 'Liberté, Egalité, Fraternité — ou Mort' was a call to arms, not just a set of demands for freedom, justice and brotherhood. But the 1940s doctrines had very different aims. Partly, they were written to limit the powers of governments, as were the earlier ones. But they were also written to define the positive roles that governments must have in shaping the societies they govern. They stated what were thought to be the *moral principles* required for the creation of a just, secure and prosperous world. The people of Europe had recently suffered two world wars, the Great Depression, and the Holocaust, and the mood everywhere was to put an end to all this suffering and evil, and to create a morally good world, in which people could live with dignity in peace and security.

Thirdly, the kind of freedom demanded in the earlier doctrines was basically just *political* liberty, i.e. freedom from domination by foreign or authoritarian governments. But in addition to political liberty, the kinds of freedom sought by the framers of the post-war human rights doctrines also included *personal freedoms*. Consider Article 22 of the *Universal Declaration*.

> Everyone, as a member of society, has the right to social security and is entitled to realization, through national effort and international co-operation and in accordance with the organization and resources of each state, of the economic, social and cultural rights *indispensable for his dignity and the free development of his personality*. (my italics)

So, the question that was being asked was this:

What do people really need, if they are to be capable of living with dignity, and developing their own personalities, in their own societies?

The succeeding Articles (23 to 29) then spell out the answers given to this question by the authors of the *Universal Declaration*.

These Articles might alternatively be called 'basic human entitlements'. Consider Article 25 (1).

> (1) Everyone has the right to a standard of living adequate for the health and well-being of himself and of his family, including food, clothing, housing and medical care and necessary social services, and the right to security in the event of unemployment, sickness, disability, widowhood, old age or other lack of livelihood in circumstances beyond his control.

This article expresses a demand for positive help on occasions of need. It is not just a demand for liberty.

In what follows, I will argue that Labor's historic mission is to create, and maintain democratically, a contemporary state based on positive human rights of the kind that Labor governments have always tried to build. Such a state was traditionally called 'a welfare state', and, in keeping with this tradition, I shall call it a welfare state too. But, as we shall see, it is a new kind of welfare state that will be required. For its economy will inevitably be largely concerned with the provision of personal and social services, in keeping with Article 25.

The philosophy of the welfare state is neither capitalist nor socialist, as these terms were understood in the nineteenth century, and is adequately described in T. Meyer (2005/2007) and B. Ellis

(2012). The state to be developed must be attuned to the world in which we live. It must, for example, be sexually, racially, and otherwise an all-inclusive welfare state, not an exclusive one like that of the 1940s. It must also be attuned to the newly emerging concepts of work and social responsibility, not just a nostalgic return to what was once the case. Moreover, it must be green and environmentally friendly. No modern democracy could possibly be anything else. And, finally, the kind of state required must be strongly egalitarian. It must not only seek to close the gap between rich and poor, it must also aim to create a society of social equals, by providing meaningful employment for everyone capable of working.

6

The Need for
Social Equality

'SOCIAL HUMANISM', which is the name I have given (in Ellis, 2012) to the underlying philosophy of the *Universal Declaration of Human Rights*, is largely about achieving *social equality*. So is Pierre Rosanvallon's groundbreaking book *A Society of Equals* (2013). Social equality is one of a number of species of equality discussed in the literature.

For social equality to exist in a given society, the members must normally be disposed to treat all others as their social equals, and so have equal concern for them as people, independently of their social status. There are some economic conceptions of equality that are based largely on the idea that people should have more or less equal incomes, wealth, or access to resources. But social equality is not an economic concept, and is not to be identified with any of these. It involves only equality of concern, treatment and respect, and it provides for 'real' equality of opportunity, which is something that will be discussed presently.

Social equality requires that concern and regard for others

should be extended to everyone. But it would require a big social movement to create and maintain such an attitude. For it is not a natural one. Human beings are naturally tribal and retributive, and therefore inclined to adopt the hierarchical social structures inherent in tribalism, and to limit their concerns for others' well-being to those they see as being like them. To counter our intuitive tribalism and vindictiveness, and to create and maintain social cohesion, it is necessary that we should demand attitudes of *social egalitarianism*, i.e. a commitment to realising a state of social equality in our own society. And this may take some time and effort.

Social equality is relationship between people that depends on how they regard and treat each other. It is not a relationship that depends crucially upon equality of wealth, income, or access to resources. Nor is it just equality in and before the law, i.e. no arbitrary discrimination in the law itself, and none in its implementation, although it implies this. Social equality also requires equality in and before the set of *all of the accepted social norms* of the society, so that, in a socially egalitarian society there is no arbitrary discrimination present in our social customs. In a socially equal society, everyone is disposed to treat all others with the same basic concern for their dignity and wellbeing. In other words, social equality implies a kind of *social contractual egalitarianism*.

Social equality may also require more honesty and civility in political debate, both in Parliament and in public. For an egalitarian culture is not likely to survive for long, if political leaders and commentators treat politics as a sort of blood sport. There is nothing basically wrong with the political party system. But there is something very wrong with many people's attitudes to political debate. A campaign for office must not be allowed to become a sort of gladiatorial contest. It should be more of a contest of ideas. But, unfortunately, there is no easy way to change these attitudes. They evolve with the culture. Ideally, there should be clear distinctions drawn between lies, honest mistakes, policy changes, broken promises and false predictions. And, every child should be taught these distinctions in school. Of these, lies are deliberate misstatements of fact or intention, and are usually reprehensible. And, normally, promises should not be made unless one is reasonably sure that one can keep them.

A society in which socially egalitarian attitudes prevail may include a few millionaires, or even billionaires. For what is most important is not wealth or income equality, but that there should be equality of respect and concern for people, independently of their wealth or income. It *does* matter that no one should be so poor, or so downtrodden, that they cannot take advantage of what is on offer, and participate fully in the social life of the community. It also matters, if some people are denied the dignity of full employment. So, some people will need support, and everyone capable of working will need a decent job. Therefore, it is important that everyone should pay his or her fair share of taxation to provide support and/or employment where it is needed.

To realise socially egalitarian attitudes in Australia need not be expensive. But it would certainly require a huge cultural change. Legislation alone probably cannot do it, because the change required is basically a moral one. And, legislation has to follow morality, not prescribe it. Nor can wealth redistribution succeed in bringing about the required changes. To create social egalitarianism the members of a society must somehow become more humanistic in their attitudes. That is, they must, as Rawls

(1971) suggested, be able and willing to abstract from their own positions and interests, and consider social issues from a purely humanistic point of view. That is, they must be able to operate socially from behind a 'veil of ignorance' concerning their own stations in life, which some people will inevitably find difficult.

Obviously, capitalism and individualism do not encourage such abstract perspectives. On the contrary, they undermine them. Free market capitalism requires us to take the viewpoint of the individual in all matters, and this is likely to lead to the gross neglect of basic *human entitlements*. Socialism requires us to adopt the viewpoint of the producers of goods and services, i.e. the workers and their managers. But, the history of the West since the nineteenth century has demonstrated that the degree of social control required to maintain a socialist regime does not make for a free or democratic society. However, we do know, from the examples of Scandinavia and Northern Europe, precisely what is required. We need a kind of welfare state in which people would normally treat each other as social equals, without having to be pressured, or required by law, to do so. That is, we need a flourishing social democracy with a strongly egalitarian social contract.

But the attitudes of social contractual egalitarianism are probably not enough by themselves to create social equality from scratch. What may be needed is a program I call one of 'real equality of opportunity'. By the creation of real equality of opportunity I mean something stronger than just the *legal* provision of equality of opportunity. Those who have been raised in disadvantaged communities, or have lived on the margins of society for many generations, may be so lacking in the confidence and the social skills that others have in abundance that they are unable, or too embarrassed, to take advantage of the opportunities available to them. Real equality of opportunity will certainly require the services of a great many professional support staff—people who are sufficiently well attuned to the problems of the individuals they are required to support. In the case of aborigines, it may require the services of aboriginal professionals who can more readily empathise with the people they have to assist.

We should not shy away from such action on the ground that it privileges some people over others. There is nothing unjust about seeking to overcome entrenched disadvantage. It is something we may have to do, if we are to create a socially egalitarian society. Most of us are accustomed to think of personal freedom in terms of what the laws or customs of our society allow us to do. But this is not a socially realistic conception of personal freedom. Realistically, we must think of ourselves as occupying a kind of choice space, which is effectively limited by what we are economically, socially and psychologically *capable* of doing. For this choice space is what really defines the range of choices that we are free to make. The philosophers Amartya Sen and Martha Nussbaum make good use of this *capability* conception of freedom, or 'practical freedom' as it might alternatively be called, in their analyses of the choices available to disadvantaged peoples everywhere. And, so should we in Australia.

7

Towards a New Welfare State

IF LABOR'S HISTORIC MISSION IS TO DEVELOP A MODERN WELFARE STATE, then we have to be clear what we want, and why we want it. A welfare state is not a compromise between socialism and capitalism, any more than a straight drive is a compromise between a hook and a slice. It has an independent and sound metaphysical foundation, which has been spelt out elsewhere (Ellis, 2012). This independent foundation is a moral one, based upon the kind of moral philosophy that generated the *Universal Declaration of Human Rights*. It is a philosophy that is based upon values of social egalitarianism (Ellis, 2012), and Benthamite social pragmatism (Collins, 1985).

It is not a transitional state. It is not to be thought of as a stage in the realisation of a fully socialist society, which owns all of the means of production, distribution, communication and exchange, although, plausibly this is how some of the left-wing intellectuals in Australia once thought of it. Nor is it like the Chinese economy, which, plausibly, many Chinese intellectuals believe is a stage in the development of a capitalist society, in which all of the means of production, distribution, communication and exchange will eventually be in private hands. No, the welfare state has its own founding document. And that document is the *Universal Declaration of Human Rights*. It does not, as Marx did, try to model society on the traditional family, with a father figure firmly in charge of everyone. Nor does it try to model society in the image of a failed economic model of a perfect market, in which there is, by definition, a God-like invisible hand guiding things to ensure that everyone prospers. The welfare state is morally structured one, which is pragmatically adapted to provide as well as possible for people's needs and aspirations. And the idea that it should be rubbished because it is just a compromise between left- and right-wing extremes is absurd.

I think it is time that all people in modern socially egalitarian states—ones that are founded upon the concepts of personal freedom and human rights—began to work together to change the world. The *Universal Declaration* of 1948 is not the last word on human rights and freedoms. Our understanding of what is morally required for a good society is constantly evolving. And, it is not to be found by looking back to the natural rights doctrines of eighteenth century, or to the neoliberal doctrines of the twentieth. The best we can do, for now, may be that we should go back to the post-war project of building a moral society on the basis of the widely agreed human rights convention of 1948, and the associated Covenants that were adopted by the United Nations in 1966. A welfare state, which embraces these concepts, and is founded upon them, is not going anywhere, unless it is forcibly taken there by bigots or lunatics. It is not inherently unstable, as the countries of Scandinavia and Northern Europe have adequately demonstrated.

But we don't want a welfare state that is locked in to the mores of the 1950s and 60s. We want a welfare state for the 21st century, where people of all social backgrounds can live and work together in reasonable harmony. There are to be no glass ceilings or other social barriers of any kind. But we do not want just an inward looking society either. If they wish, people must be able to participate, not only as equals within their own societies, but also as equals in other sophisticated societies around the world.

8

Australia's Post-war Welfare State

When Ben Chifley was made prime minister, following the fatal illness of John Curtin, Australia already had many of the ingredients of a welfare state. The State and Federal Governments between them owned most of the infrastructure and public utilities (electricity generation, water, power lines, postal services, railways, roads and so on). So, there was no need to nationalise them, as there had been in the UK. Much of this ownership went back to the colonial days. But this did not save the Australian economy from being devastated by the Great Depression of the 1930s, because no one at that time knew how to deal with this phenomenon. Nevertheless, our economically depressed nation was not, as a result, prevented from contributing very substantially to the war effort from 1939 onwards. And this experience, like the experience of the British, convinced most Australians that 'if, through hard work and cooperation, we could win the war, then we could also win the peace'. So Ben Chifley began his term in office convinced that through hard work and cooperation,

Australia would be able to construct a new social order, in which poverty would be eliminated, and people would receive welfare and assistance throughout their lives, as the need arose.

For those of you who never knew, or have forgotten, what the welfare state of the Chifley to Whitlam period was like, let me remind you.

1. It was a time of genuinely full employment. In Australia, unemployment averaged 2.0 % from 1953 to 1974. And, these were not phoney figures, constructed to make governments look good. They were real.

2. Real GDP growth (1960–1974) averaged 5.2 % per annum.

3. Inflation rate (1960–1974) averaged 3.3 % per annum.

4. Hourly wage rates at every level (from the poorest quintile to the richest) kept pace with productivity growth from 1945 to 1975.

5. Public and private debt were both well managed and under control. In fact, current account deficits were miniscule or non-existent until 1980.[11] [12]

6. The Chifley Government was frustrated in its efforts to construct a more prosperous welfare state than the rudimentary one it inherited. Chifley's bill to nationalise the banks was declared unconstitutional, as was his health-care legislation. Nevertheless, Chifley is remembered for his inspirational leadership, the Snowy Mountains Scheme, the ANU, the Holden car, full employment, soldier resettlement, education reform, and

for getting Australia's economy moving again, apparently to nearly everyone's advantage.

7. The Menzies government, although much more conservative than Chifley's, worked with a similar conception of the role of the state in society. It was a social liberal conception. But it was strongly against bank nationalisation, and, like other conservative governments a bit afraid of the direction in which Chifley appeared to be moving, a concern that became increasingly worrying as the Cold War developed. Nevertheless, Menzies' government considerably improved Australia's educational provisions for young people, and did not try to undo the welfare state which then existed.

8. It was left to the Whitlam government to introduce free university education, establish a constitutionally acceptable national health service (Medibank),[13] and definitively establish Australia as an advanced welfare state.

The welfare state of the Chifley era was a product of its time, and, by today's standards, it was protectionist, racist and sexist. But, while the state that was established in the Whitlam era was still protectionist, it was formally neither sexist nor racist. Indeed, Whitlam took all of the basic steps needed to transform our society into a socially all-inclusive egalitarian one. Unfortunately, we are still in process of making this transition.

The welfare state was also ecologically extravagant, and was built on the assumption that the world's oceans and atmosphere are virtually infinite, and so ultimately indestructible. Any new welfare state that might now be built must be one that is not

45

only socially all-inclusive and egalitarian. It must also be one that is conscious of the need to preserve, and live in harmony with, our natural environment. It must, in short, be a green, inclusive, socially egalitarian welfare state.

It became clear during the Second World War that Australia could no longer rely upon Britain to protect it militarily. Evatt sought security under the umbrella of the United Nations. But, with the developing Cold War, this too became untenable, and Australia formally became strategically dependent upon the United States under the ANZUS Treaty, even though this treaty is, in reality, nothing more than an agreement to consult in the event of an emerging threat.

Malcolm Fraser (2014) has argued persuasively that Australia's strategic dependence upon the United States has now become a paradox. He says:

> Our leaders argue we need to keep our alliance with the United States strong in order to ensure our defence in the event of an aggressive foe. Yet the most likely reason Australia would need to confront an aggressive foe is our strong alliance with the United States. (p. 257)

So, for all of Fraser's reasons, our policy of strategic dependence upon the US must now be abandoned. We can be allies, but we must develop as a strategically independent nation, with its traditions firmly planted in Australian history and culture.

Therefore, we must be able to do what we think is right, rather than what is expedient. We can agree to consult with America, when there appears to be instability developing in our region, just as the ANZUS Treaty requires. But we cannot be drawn unnecessarily into conflicts that do not pose serious threats to our existence. A welfare state for the 21st century must, therefore, be strategically independent, as well as green, inclusive, and socially egalitarian.

In creating the first welfare state, Chifley fought hard to distance himself, and his government, from the communist beliefs and attitudes that influenced the early trade union movement in Australia. He was a centrist, in the sense that he believed in centralising power in Canberra. But he was also a democrat, not a Marxist or Leninist. Consequently, the communist leaders of several of Australia's trade unions regarded Mr. Chifley's program as a sell-out to capitalism. The 'pure' position they advocated required a revolution, a dictatorship of the proletariat, and state ownership and control of 'all of the means of production, distribution and exchange—not just a continuation of the democratic process. But what they got was 'reformism', as they mockingly called it, not the kind of change they all wanted. And, in 1949, the Miner's Federation, which was strongly influenced by the Communist Party of Australia, brought 23,000 coal miners out on strike, and challenged the authority of the Federal Government by continuing the strike in defiance of Chifley's sincere attempts at reconciliation. In frustration, Chifley ordered 2,500 troops in to work the open cut mines in Minmi, Musswellbrook and Ben Bullen to break the strike, thus staking his authority as Prime Minister on the outcome. Mr Chifley won this battle, but, with divisions in his own party, he lost the general election in December later that year, and Mr Menzies was elected to power.

The philosophical basis of the modern welfare state is manifestly not Marxist or Leninist. It is socially humanistic. Specifically, it is the socially egalitarian humanism of the *Universal Declaration of the Human Rights*, and, if you believe in this doctrine, or any of the other human rights documents of the time, then you ought also to believe in the welfare state, because you cannot consistently have one without the other. A welfare state for the 21st century must therefore be a strategically independent, green, inclusive, social egalitarian welfare state that is unaligned with the forces of either communism or capitalism.

9

Towards the Creation of a New Welfare State

To begin this process, we must get people back to work, and motivate them to create a good, stable and sustainable future for our children and grandchildren. And, if there is a will to do this, then there will be a way. For, states of the kind we must build have already been created. It is just up to us to create our own special version of it, and adapt it to the traditions and needs of our own culture.

The primary problem is that there does not appear to be enough work for Australian workers to do. According to the Australian Bureau of Statistics, unemployment in Australia averaged 6.91 percent from 1980 until 2014, reaching a high of 10.90 percent in December of 1992[14], and a low of 4.1 percent in February of 2008, just before the GFC began to have serious effects here. Moreover, there does not seem to be much prospect of there being enough work in future to keep us busy. It is not that

Australia has been in recession. The problem existed long before the Global Financial Crisis of 2008, which only made it worse. Full employment, as it once existed in Australia, has not existed anywhere in the world, as far as I know, since the mid-seventies. From 1953 to 1973, the Australian unemployment averaged 2.0%. And, unemployment in Australia stood officially at less than 3% for almost the whole of the post-war boom. By comparison, no rich country, anywhere, has had anything like full employment since the early seventies.

Yet the economies of wealthy countries have all enjoyed positive growth rates for almost twenty years. So, chronic unemployment is not just a recent phenomenon. High unemployment of 6% or more, and much higher under-employment rates, are endemic to all modern capitalist societies. To deal with unemployment, and under-employment, the strategy adopted early in the eighties was to expand the economy rapidly, by: (a) floating the currency, (b) removing tariff barriers, subsidies, and other impediments to free trade, (c) making it easier and cheaper for people to borrow money, and (d) selling government assets. But this strategy built up huge private debts, and created an insecure, internally highly competitive, society, which was dominated by a hyper-rich class, a wealthy upper middle-class, a struggling lower-middle class, and a poor and dispirited working class.

More recently, the emphasis has shifted to creating free trade agreements (FTAs), and this year (2014) at the G20 Summit in Brisbane, Australia struck an historic free trade agreement with China, as a follow-up to its free trade deals with North America, Japan and South Korea, and is now engaged with India in drawing up a free trade agreement with them. All of this is being done in the belief that: (a) businesses are the best creators of jobs,

(b) the freer the trade, the more business activity there will be, and (c) rapid economic growth will overcome the problem of joblessness.

But businesses are not notably good at creating jobs. They employ as few people as possible, and only employ them on projects that provide them with adequate returns. Fair enough. But the fact remains that businesses are strongly motivated to: (a) minimise their workforces, (b) replace tenured staff with casuals, (c) workers by machinery, (d) manufacture things overseas wherever suitable labour is cheaper, and (e) import manufactured parts rather than commission local firms to manufacture them. Hence, if governments are not prepared to spend on behalf of the community on social goods and services, then the national economy has to grow considerably faster than the numbers seeking employment, if it is to satisfy the social demand for work.

Unfortunately, the market-driven economies of the world's wealthiest nations have not been able to create this much demand on their own—even with free trade deals. They spend billions on advertising to try to generate enough demand for things—often for things that hardly anyone wants. Yet, despite their best efforts, large pools of unemployed remain.

But, such are the marketing opportunities likely to be created by the deals with Japan, China, India and South Korea, that this round of FTAs may well succeed in clearing some of the backlog of unemployed people in Australia. I hope so. But, even if it is successful, it will almost certainly be at the cost of (a) what remains of our manufacturing industries, (b) our ownership of Australian resources, (and hence our national self-reliability), and (c) our responsibilities to those who have been injured by past neoliberal programs.

These are all problems that need to be considered. A nation without significant manufacturing industries for supplying world markets (other than wine-making, perhaps) is necessarily a very dependent one. The free trade agreements we have already signed would commit us to living in a society with virtually no labour-intensive industries. And any internationally marketable goods or services that we could possibly make in Australia, but which could be supplied by an FTA partner, almost certainly will be supplied by one of them more cheaply than we could supply it ourselves.[15] Therefore, we must, in all of these ways, become dependent upon our FTA partners.

Moreover, a nation without significant manufacturing industries is one with only a narrow range of employment opportunities. It makes the unskilled and blue-collar workers and their female counterparts more or less redundant, and, if they cannot adequately be retrained to become technologically proficient, or socially useful in some other way, then the range of employment opportunities available to them in a society such as ours must be become inadequate. The FTAs are therefore likely to result in very high unemployment rates in this group. At first, this can be expected to give rise to anger and resentment. But, in the longer term, if neoliberal philosophy prevails politically, then it is likely to turn into bitterness and frustration, and cause all of the social and mental disorders that characterise the chronically unemployed poor in all modern capitalist societies.

Finally, a nation that willingly enters into free trade agreements that are likely to cause even more people in our society to feel cast out of any constructive role must face up to the fact that the group that is most likely to be affected is the one that is already the most threatened. Consequently, the task of treating, rehabilitating, and re-engaging those who have already fallen by the wayside, e.g. by becoming depressed or addicted to drugs, will probably be made all the more difficult.

Therefore, the FTA with China, which was announced at the G20 Summit recently, is not all a bed of roses. It demands that we put aside most of the profits arising from our investments in China, and many of the savings we will make on Chinese goods and services supplied to Australia, in order to provide for the wellbeing of those who are most likely to suffer displacement as a result. The benefits of these deals must not be allowed to flow only to those with money to spend, while those who have lost their jobs must just sit by and watch others enjoy the benefits for which their jobs have been sacrificed. The government has a clear moral duty to promote the wellbeing and dignity of all Australians, not just look after the already wealthy or technologically highly competent sections of the community.

On the other hand, free trade appears to have been a boon to the poor and underdeveloped countries of the world. It has lifted their productivity (as measured by GDP per capita) to unprecedented heights (Michael Spence, 2011). We should not, therefore, abandon the laudable aims of globalisation, unless we are: (a) convinced that there is no viable alternative, and (b) prepared to take strong action to support any developing countries that might be adversely affected by required new trade restrictions. Free trade is certainly good for business, and it appears to be good for the poor countries of the world, where wages are low and conditions poor.

My colleague, Hugh Lacey,[16] has commented:

> As I look at recent history in Brazil, there is some truth in this—once poor people have been re-

moved from the land and pushed into slums, and into doing work for little pay and under terrible conditions, free trade does contribute to bettering the lives of large numbers of them.

But he goes on to say that 'for many of them, being pushed into these conditions in the first place was itself a consequence of free trade practices—it involved an impoverishment of their lives, and the elimination of the hope that they had for their lives, based in improving forms of agriculture'.

This may well be so. But it seems to me that the sub-policy of exporting our manufacturing, packing and assembling industries to third world countries was not *inherently* bad for these countries. Its ill effects in Brazil were due to the exploitation of rural people by home grown capitalists, not the ill effects of globalization. However, I concede that globalization is not unquestionably 'a boon to the developing world', as Spence would say. It is at best only a qualified good.

But globalization is certainly against the interests of the unskilled and blue-collar workers of the rich world. It puts many of them out of a job, and does nothing to help them find a new one. And, this is a consequence that globalization is directly responsible for. It has stripped these workers in the rich world of nearly all of the benefits their ancestors struggled so hard, for so many years, to achieve through union activity, and forced them to accept lower wages, and much poorer working conditions, than they would otherwise have had.

But restrictive trade practices cannot now be imposed without great risk of bad economic consequences, not to mention the possibility of economic sanctions. Therefore, I think that there is really only one practical way to proceed, if we want to create full employment for, and restore the dignity of, Australia's currently under-employed working class. We must return to the tried and true policies that led to the establishment of the first welfare state in Australia, and its further development under Gough Whitlam, and take it from there into this present century.

10

The Problem of Unemployment

To do this properly, we have to be clear about the nature of the problem of unemployment that we are seeking to solve. The problem is this: our business community is either unable or unwilling to provide enough employment of the required kinds. An average unemployment rate of 6.9% for the 35 years from 1979 to 2014 is simply not good enough. In the post-war boom, this level of unemployment would have been considered scandalous. Unemployment exceeded 3% only once in the 30 year period from 1945 to 1975, when it soared to just over 3% in 1961, and almost cost Mr. Menzies his job.[17] It can be said that two income households and women in the workforce make the task of creating full employment much more difficult. But Australia is an immigrant country, and we have absorbed more than seven million immigrants in the 70 years since 1945. It beggars belief that we could not just as easily have absorbed the ten percent increase in the percentage of women in the workforce (46% to 56%) that has occurred in the period from 1978 to 2012.[18]

Indeed, it is rather disturbing, because, over the same period, the percentage of men in the workforce decreased from 80% to 72%, which suggests that women are either replacing men in the workforce, or that women are much more competitive for the kinds of jobs that are on offer, and that many men have simply withdrawn, or have been forced out of the work force. Probably, the cause is a combination of these two factors. And, even the average unemployment rate of 6.9% since 1979, which is monstrous, disguises the depth of the human tragedy this represents.

It may, indeed, be the case that the kinds of jobs that are likely to become available in the private sector are more likely to favor women than men. The near disappearance of our traditional manufacturing industries, and the replacement of manual work by machines, have greatly reduced job opportunities for unskilled labor and blue-collar workers. So, any new welfare state will need to promote industries that develop good prospects for male employment.

Manifestly, businesses are not providing enough employment to create job opportunities for everyone, male or female. Businesses may ultimately be able to satisfy the needs of working women, because the kinds of work that are likely to become available in the next generation or so will probably favour them. But, with current policy settings, it seems unlikely they will be able to satisfy the needs of working men, whatever happens.

In the industrialized societies of the twentieth century, most men defined their lives by what they did for a living, and most women defined theirs by their roles as mothers or homemakers. But all this began to change in the 1970s. Women were demanding, and are now in process of getting, social equality with men—a process that has yet to be completed. But, for the 21st

century, we must suppose that social equality will eventually be achieved.

This change will inevitably have profound consequences for the nature of work. Before the change, men were assumed to be the breadwinners for their families. Therefore, they could devote themselves to their work without having to negotiate their responsibilities with their partners. The responsibilities were already divided by convention. But, in the 21st century, this will not be a reasonable assumption. Men will usually have to negotiate with their partners to determine in what ways, and to what extent, their public careers and their private home duties are to be divided. And this, in turn, implies that most men will no longer be able to identify with their public careers in quite the way they did, and that women will not be forced to accept many of the responsibilities of home duties that men and their mothers-in-law used to take for granted. Obviously, it will be an exciting world for women. For they will be able to use their talents to make their mark in society through their work and achievements, much more than they ever have in the past. But, for many men, especially working-class men, it may well be tragic. And it seems that their problems are likely to increase, unless there is a concerted effort to find suitable work for them to do.

As social equality increases in the workforce, the workforces of the future seem likely to become less and less male-dominated, and could even become female-dominated. For the primary needs of wealthy societies like ours now lie in the provision of services. And, most of the services that will inevitably be needed, and needed increasingly, are ones that have traditionally been provided by women. The areas that especially need to be developed are childcare, early learning, and aged care, and all of them will need to grow considerably for the next generation or two. Childcare and early learning need to grow because more women are working, and more of them will wish to return to work fairly soon after their children are born. And, aged care needs to develop (a) because this area has been neglected, and (b) because people are living longer now than ever before. Indeed, the proportion of women in the workforce seems likely to become similar to that of men in the not too distant future.

To develop a socially equal society, in which men and women have equal opportunities in the workforce, we must aim to create social equality where it counts most—in the management structures of the nation. To achieve this result, men and women will have to have roughly equal market power. They must have comparably good educations and training, roughly equal wealth, and real equality of opportunity for appointments and promotions to or within all management structures. At present, they have none of these. Therefore, if social equality in the workplace is a primary objective for our new welfare state, as it should be, we will need to begin with the kinds of technical and moral education that will be required to achieve this result.

Traditionally, moral education has been left to the churches. But the moral perspectives of Christians, Muslims, Jews, Hindus and Bhuddists are significantly different from one another, especially in their beliefs about the role and status of women in society. If, as I have argued, social humanism is the moral philosophy of the welfare state, and also of the *Universal Declaration of Human Rights*, then any new development of a welfare state would require either a secular society, or a dominant religion in which gender egalitarianism is acceptable.

Against this, it might be argued that religious beliefs, whatever they might be, are more fundamental than any secular morality. Consequently, we may just have to accept that different religions support different moral systems, and therefore different social systems, and, consequently, that the requirement of social equality cannot reasonably be demanded. But, as Plato argued convincingly in the Euthyphro, religiously founded moral beliefs are not primary. Secular morality, he argued, should be primary—even among the devoutly religious. So, if a state wishes to defend gender equality in the workforce, then the morality of gender equality must be hammered out in the community. Probably, the question of gender equality should be thoroughly discussed in schools everywhere by professional ethicists—or at least by people who are well-trained in moral philosophy. For, if we are to develop a culture of social equality in the workplace, then we must at least be clear what it means, and what its implications are. It could turn out, for all I know, that social equality in the workplace is ultimately compatible with every mainstream religious belief system. But, at present, that seems unlikely.

In any case, the current trend toward social equality between men and women in the workplace is probably now irresistible. Therefore, we must prepare ourselves for the social upheaval that it will cause. In the 21st century, men and women will be just as likely as one another to have public careers. So, a whole new set of problems of personal compatibility are bound to arise in family relationships. Men will no longer be able to assume that they can pursue their careers in the way that they have in the past, and for the most part still do. Women, on the other hand, will normally have to negotiate with their husbands as to whether, and if so when, they may have children, and who will care for them. For, the choices they make will impact on them both, and also on their public careers.

A person's public career can give meaning to his or her life. Therefore, it is important for the social health of a country that all employees should be able to develop their skills, and establish careers in the kind of work they do. Consequently, when we speak of equality of opportunity, this should be what we have in mind—*equality of career opportunity*. To promote such an ideal, there is clearly a need for us to develop an educational system that is geared to achieving it, and a social system that aims to create new career opportunities. A career in a specific science, for example, not only requires that there should be people who are well-educated in the specific science in question. It also requires that the society provides career opportunities for those who are well-educated in the field. There is, therefore, an important difference between the bare provision of employment and that of providing genuine career opportunities. Dead-end employment is employment that is not intended to lead to anything beyond itself. It might suit a person who is temporarily out of work, or wishes to gain experience, or to make some money. Or it might allow an employer to fill a temporary staff vacancy. But the offer of a dead-end job cannot be compared with one of an ongoing position in an organization in which there is career potential.

Equality of access to career opportunities does, of course, require equality of access to career-type jobs. But, strictly speaking, it implies much more than this. Firstly, it requires that our appointments procedures should not be biased in favor of anyone other than those who are best qualified for the positions to be filled. It also requires that, if specialist education is required for the position to be filled, then access to such education should be available to all, and, if there is a selection process involved in admissions to such courses, then all such processes must select on the basis of merit. Secondly, career opportunities can arise in business enterprises. If a person seeks a career in business, then he or she is unlikely to get very far without being able to set up a business of their own, or set one up in partnership with others. Therefore, if the principle of equality of career opportunities is accepted, there must be procedures in our society for teaching people how to go about this, how to make a business case for a project one has in mind, how to obtain access to an appropriate level of start-up capital for a speculative venture, and how to manage the business when it is established. Moreover, these procedures must be open to everyone, and be selective of the best-qualified applicants, without gender bias, or social bias toward any particular social group.

To create such opportunities, it would probably be necessary to create business studies streams in state school curricula, provide scholarships to tertiary-level business colleges, and make grants of start-up capital available to successful graduates from these colleges.

For these reasons, work in the 21st century seems likely to focus on the need for career jobs, i.e. jobs that people can take in the reasonable hope of building careers for themselves in the kinds of businesses or organizations that employ them, or in which they themselves become employers. Of course, some people will have the social confidence, or family backing, to strike out on their own, e.g. by establishing business enterprises, or becoming self-employed, e.g. as entrepreneurs, artists, or authors, and develop career paths for themselves. But, most people must inevitably be employed by others in business or government organizations, and work, as best they can, to establish careers for themselves in these organizations. The big problem then is that there are currently not enough jobs of the required kinds being generated in the wealthy countries of the world to meet the demand for them. So, governments will have to step in to provide them, if they cannot ensure that sufficient numbers of such jobs will be made available commercially.

The kinds of jobs that are urgently required now, and will certainly be required in much larger numbers in future, are career jobs—*real* jobs, as some people like to say—i.e. jobs that offer at least continuing employment, and preferably also prospects for advancement. Such jobs were provided in abundance in the post-war boom. The question is: Where are such jobs now to be found?

11

Work in the Provision of Services

ALL PAID WORK IS SERVICE. It is action to make or do something that is valued. All employers are agents who hire people to perform such actions. All action to make or do things is said by economists to be productive, even though some of the things produced may be toxic, and some of the actions done may be destructive.

In discussing production, economists have traditionally distinguished between goods and services. Goods were supposed to be substantial things that the employers can own, and do more or less what they like with. Services were thought to be actions that are valued by an employer, but which the employer cannot own. The distinction has become a bit muddied lately with the development of the so-called 'knowledge industry'. But this crude picture will do for the purposes of this essay.

The prices that employers pay for the goods and services they purchase is taken to be the measure of their value to the employer. But goods, being enduring objects, may be sold on to other purchasers. So, most goods also have a retail value. The sum total of the money paid for the goods and services sold in any one year may be considerably greater than the money that is paid to the workers who produced these goods and services. Nevertheless, the monetary value (as measured by their sale prices in a given year) of all of the finished goods and services produced within a country's borders in that year is an important measure of the country's economic activity. It is known as the 'Gross Domestic Product' or GDP.

The productivity of a state is normally measured by its GDP per capita. But GDP and productivity are not neutral measures of anything other than the level of business activity. There are other measures that might be used to measure productivity—e.g. measures that focus on local production that is socially desirable. Obviously, the standard definition of productivity would be attractive to those who think that happiness lies just in maximising GDP. However, our wellbeing also depends on how goods and services are distributed, as Joseph Stiglitz (2012) has convincingly demonstrated.

To create full employment in Australia, it is clear that jobs must be created in the areas of social and personal services. For these are the areas that have been most neglected in the neoliberal era. Mental health care is one such area. The closure of most of the old mental hospitals in Australia was welcome. But the new arrangements for mental health care are still unsatisfactory. Mental health care normally requires continuing supervision and support in a positive and homely environment. And, inevitably, this must sometimes require residence in an appropriate home, where such ambience can be provided. But this does not appear to have been the common practice. Too many young men and women were returned to their original home environments, with prescription drugs to suppress their symptoms, and provided with professional contacts, should they need further support. But, in retrospect, this was an attempt to buy mental health treatment on the cheap, and allow the government of the day to capitalise on the sale of the (often very valuable) land on which the original mental hospitals were located. It is encouraging that the Liberal and Labor parties are now united behind a national plan for care of the mentally ill, which attempts to address some of the real problems.

A second area of neglect has been that of addiction. The war on drugs, which we have been pursuing as a national policy for many years, has been a social disaster. It has led to the establishment of powerful networks of organized crime, the creation of a clientele of highly dependent drug addicts scattered throughout the country, and the consequent dysfunctionality of many country towns and suburbs. What is needed is an end to the war on drugs, and to legalise the public manufacture and distribution of drugs, or substitute drugs, to addicts who agree to rehabilitation, and the establishment of drug treatment and rehabilitation centres in or near to all affected country towns and suburbs.

Thirdly, old people need services. It is highly desirable that they should be able to remain in their own homes and neighbourhoods for as long as possible. Keeping them there in tolerable conditions will require an army of carers and assistants—people who can not only provide personal assistance to old people with bathing, cleaning, cooking, washing, and so on, but also some who can provide home assistance to maintain paths, gardens, gutters, sheds, fittings, fences, and the like. And, this need will increasingly become urgent as the percentage of old people in the community increases. I would suggest that every town and suburb should have a home help centre, where workers in the various categories of assistance are registered and approved, and where subsidized help can be provided where it is needed.

A fourth area of neglect has been clean energy. We should now be training a whole army of people competent in the various fields of low-carbon technology. For, this is where much future employment must lie. But instead of steering students into these fields, the Government appears to be steering them away from them. Indeed, there is a sort of suspicion of science generally in the governing parties. There is no science minister in the present Government of Australia. And there is no special focus on science, mathematics, design or technology in schools. In fact, education generally, and technical education in particular, have been sabotaged by the Howard government's ideological promotion of private education at the expense of public education. Private schools are good at producing lawyers, business people and politicians. But public schools have always been very productive of scientists and engineers, who, as I have argued in *Rationalism* (2015), are the real generators of the wealth of nations.

The anti-science stance of the present neoliberal government has left the country dangerously out of touch with current technical developments. Strictly speaking, there is no good reason why this anti-science stance should have been taken. It does not follow from the argument for remaking society in the image of a neoclassical perfect market. For, there is no reason why the residents of a perfect market should avoid research and development in science and technology, or in any other area. On the contrary, if you really believe that selling things creates wealth, you should also give some thought why people would want to buy them. And, basically, people want to buy things, not because they are being offered for sale, but because they are technically better, or better designed, than other similarly priced things on offer. Therefore, you should also be in favour of (a) developing technically better things, and (b) designing them better, and (c) promoting the learning facilities that produce the people who can achieve these results.

Another reason, which may resonate with some economists, is the idea that businessmen are the real drivers of economic growth—not the scientists, technicians, designers, or other creative people who make things, but the business people who invest their money in them. They are the 'lifters', they say, who do the hard work of developing the economy. But, as I have argued elsewhere (Ellis, 2015), science and technology are the true sources of economic growth; business men and women are just the opportunists who make money out of them. Scientists and technologists are not the meek servants of industry, even if some of them are employed by industry. They are the creative ones, who are the real forces behind industrial development and growth. And, they are the ones who have powered all of the industrial revolutions in history, and the ones who will assuredly power the next one.

A fifth area has been in that of low-carbon energy technologies. Instead of urging entrepreneurs and researchers to develop these technologies for Australia, so that we could be ahead of the game, the present government has done all it could to hinder developments in this area. Consequently, important business opportunities have almost certainly been lost. We could, for example have developed wind-, wave- and solar-power technologies, while the opportunities were still there, and sold them to the world. But instead we chose to pretend that anthropogenic global warming was not happening. Any new ALP government would still have to invest heavily in low-carbon technologies. But the chances are that we have lost the golden opportunity we had in the seventies and eighties, when it first became evident to most scientists that global warming would probably occur as a result of carbon pollution.

Other areas of neglect include public education and technical training; the creation and maintenance of good public facilities for recreation and tourism; the creating and maintaining of first rate science, mathematics, music, literature, and language teaching in state schools. But it is beyond the scope of what is intended in this paper to try to list all of the things that a new welfare state might wish to do. Here, I can only try to spell out the guiding principles.

To pay for these jobs, and all of the training that will be required to staff these projects, we will certainly need a range of new tax measures. At present the primary tax burden in every advanced economy is borne by those who are in the lower to upper-middle ranges of the wages scale. This will probably always be the case. Those who are wealthy enough to afford high-powered tax accountants will have to pay their accountants, of course. But they will never have to pay much in the way of tax. So there is little to be gained by trying to tax the wealthy to pay for the reforms that are needed, unless we levy a wealth tax. For the very wealthy are not going to be able to argue successfully that they are not wealthy. There is also nothing to be gained by trying to curry favour with these people. The strategy I would recommend is to stop all private/public partnerships, and start behaving like a government that is playing hard-ball, as the Chinese government does. A government with a dedicated public service, staffed by engineers, business professionals and neo-Keynesian economists, which was prepared to use its market power to borrow money cheaply, build infrastructure, and establish the required social service centres, could quickly return dividends to those who would have to pay for it all.

The very wealthy in our community do not pay much at all in the way of income taxes, and probably never will. Nor should we employ multinational corporations, which routinely shift profits to offshore tax havens to avoid having to pay Australian taxes. We must cut them all dead, and not do business with any of them. For, the sovereign risk of massive tax evasion is much too great for us to take. Wherever possible, we should employ local companies to do the heavy lifting, or foreign companies whose past tax-paying behaviour in Australia and elsewhere poses no substantial threat.

***

Tony Judt begins the Introduction to his book *Ill Fares the Land* (2010) with these words:

Something is profoundly wrong with the way we live today. For thirty years we have made a virtue of the pursuit of material self-interest: indeed, this very pursuit now constitutes whatever remains of our sense of collective purpose. We know what things cost but have no idea of what they are worth. We no longer ask of a judicial ruling or a legislative act: is it good? Is it fair? Is it just? Is it right? Will it bring about a better society or a better world? Those used to be the political questions,

even if they invited no easy answers. We must learn
once again to pose them.

However, the problem is not just that we have forgotten how to pose these questions. Our lack of social moral concern is only another symptom of the disease. If most people have lost their social consciences, as Judt believes, then it is society that is sick, not just the individual. A society in which a great many people lack a social conscience is no longer a healthy society. It cannot function as it should, because a good society needs a clear sense of direction, a shared understanding of what would be needed to make it better, and how, roughly, to go about trying to achieve it. The disease to which Judt refers is, therefore, not fundamentally a mental disorder. It is a social disorder. We have a dysfunctional society in which all of these problems arise. And, it is this dysfunction that needs to be addressed.

Yet, I do not think that Judt's ultimate diagnosis of the problem is wrong. For the title of his book says it all. Fundamentally it is the society—'the land', he says—that 'fares ill'. And the diseases from which people suffer are all ones that many people would suffer from in any sick society. And, this is precisely what he goes on to argue. So, he is right, I think: that the whole society is sick, not just the individuals who are sickened by it. To deal with these individuals, we will, of course, have to treat them as individuals. But, more fundamentally, we are going to have to work on society—making it better, and more friendly, for people to live and work in, enabling people to relate more easily to each other, to find jobs that suit them, and to discover ways of living that are satisfying, challenging, exciting, or whatever it is that they might want out of life. It is not the individual that needs to adjust to a life in which there is not enough decent work to go around, or has no accommodation that they can afford, or no social services that they can tap into when they are in need. A society that creates, and does nothing to deal with, these deficiencies is a sick society. And this, basically, is what needs to be fixed.

Judt argues that (as of 2010) the USA and the UK are two of the most socially dysfunctional societies in the developed world. To develop the argument, he presents a number of studies linking national income inequality in the developed world with various plausible indicators of social ill-health, viz: (a) social mobility (b) health and social problems, (c) homicides, and (d) mental illness. These studies all show that the US is by far the worst in all of these respects—right off the scale in the cases of health and homicide. The UK, he points out, is also up there, vying with one or two other countries for the position of being second worst. He concludes, plausibly, that Britain and the US are both very sick societies.

In his opening chapter, Judt makes a number of other claims, which seem to point to the same conclusion. The healthiest societies in the world, he argues, are, by almost every measure, the Scandinavian countries, Japan, and the northern European social democracies. Australia, Canada and New Zealand used to be up there in this group, but have begun to slide down the scale, since they elected neoliberal governments, and began dismantling their welfare states. Dramatically, he points out that the US spends vast sums on health care, but that 'life-expectancy in the US remains below Bosnia, and just above Albania' (p. 20). Also, he makes the point that, if social mobility is accurately measured by the extent to which a son's income is not explained by his father's, then social mobility has decreased by about 33% since 1980, which, of course, is just when the neoliberal era began.

The real driver of these social ills in the US and UK was probably the grotesque income and wealth inequalities that their systems generated, and the lamentable failure of the wealthy and middle-income people in society to respect the economic and social rights of the poor. It is one thing to be rich (i.e. 'be lifters', as Joe Hockey says). It is quite another for the well-off to blame the poor for the plight they (the poor) are in (e.g. calling them 'leaners'). When there are not enough jobs to go around, someone has to miss out. And, that in itself is bad enough. But for those who succeed in the brutal competition for jobs, or those who do not need them, it is outrageous that they should be urging their governments to dismantle the social security systems upon which many of these people have become unavoidably dependent. The entitlements that Mr Hockey wishes to deny them are 'indispensable to their *dignity*, and for the *free development of their personalities*', which is precisely how Article 22 of the *Universal Declaration of Human Rights* describes them).

The framers of the *UDHR* were very clear about this. For, there is no doubt that the authors of this document set out to define a kind of society in which people would be able to live with dignity and social security. They did not describe a *laissez faire* capitalist state. Nor did they describe a communist one. Rather, they described something that was very much more like the welfare states and social democracies that began to flourish around the world in early the post-war period. It should come as no surprise, therefore, that the deliberate attempt by the present Treasurer to dismantle Australia's social and economic security provisions is clearly in defiance of Articles 22 to 28 of the *UDHR*, and therefore in breach of the UN Charter.

12

What is to be Done?

A WELFARE STATE FOR THE 21ST CENTURY MUST BE *ANTI-DISCRIMINATORY*, BOTH NATIONALLY AND INTERNATIONALLY, and embrace an economic system that compatible with the kind of globally connected world in which we now live. At the national level, it must work to achieve *social equality*, legislating social contractual egalitarian policies, but, where necessary, employing reverse discriminatory strategies to break down barriers. At the international level, the aim must be to achieve *practical equality of developmental opportunity*. That is, every country should be able to: (a) develop its own social or political systems in accordance with international agreements on human rights, entitlements, and social responsibilities, and (b) develop industries suitable for their citizens in their own environments.

Restrictions on trade and commerce are incompatible with unrestricted globalization. But there are obvious difficulties in accepting any genuinely universal free trade agreements. The difficulties result from the accidental but inherent inequalities of nation states, i.e. differences in their populations, resources, climates, locations, stages of development, and so on, which will inevitably limit the capacities of nation states to compete fairly on international markets. Some will be very strong, and able to force down prices in their favour (if they are buying), or force up prices in their favour (if they are selling). Such differences exist, for example, between the states of the Commonwealth of Australia. Some have vast mineral resources, others have very little; some have rich grazing lands, others have none to speak of; some have large populations, others small; some have large urban centres, others have none; and so on. Inevitably, these differences will entail that states have different economic strengths and weaknesses, and so could not compete as equals in an open market. Some nation states would inevitably become richer and more diverse; while others would be more or less restricted to specific tasks.

The neoliberal objective of global free trade is therefore untenable in a world of independent nation states. Free global markets are no more likely to be fair distributors of wealth and opportunities than free national markets. Hence, there would need also to be a supranational mechanism for redistributing wealth and opportunities between states. But it seems to me unlikely that any powerful state would be willing to tolerate the existence of such a mechanism. Therefore, international trade must be regulated by world bodies, which are charged with the responsibility of ensuring that international trade is fair and reasonable. The point is that the kinds of lives that people would be able to live under conditions of global free trade, would, necessarily, be dependent upon the resources of each state, and the accidents of its climate, location, and so on. Therefore, to achieve practical equality of developmental opportunity, some trade restrictions must inevitably be set in place by supranational authority.

A welfare state for the 21st century must also aim to provide high quality education for all, with the aim of providing maximum opportunity for personal fulfilment, just as welfare states have always done. But, in the special circumstances that now exist, it has become urgent that we should: (a) reform our education system to make it more egalitarian, and more readily pursued through tertiary level, and (b) greatly improve our records in teaching science and mathematics. The first of these objectives was neglected, and sometimes even opposed, in the neoliberal era. And the second has become urgent, because science and mathematics have manifestly become the principal drivers of wealth creation in the neoliberal era.[19] Moreover, combating and adapting to climate change will require the development of a whole raft of new technologies, and it is clearly important that any nation state with its eye on the future must prepare for it.

The new welfare state must aim for genuinely full employment of its citizens. It must at least: (a) try to provide as many career-type jobs as possible for tomorrow's students, and (b) seek to establish *equality of career opportunities* in employment. For these are the kinds of employment that we will need, and the kinds of opportunities that a welfare state must try to provide.

Because of the neglect of social goods in the neoliberal era, it has also become urgent that we should attend to these areas of neglect, and take corrective action. We should, for example, seek to establish social service and work-care centres in the suburbs and towns of the nation, with a view to keeping old people in their own homes as long as possible, or helping those, who, for whatever reason, need assistance to cope adequately in their own homes. These centres need to be well staffed and trained to deal with the kinds of problems that old or infirm people are likely to face, and as tactful and helpful in their assistance as possible. Some such centres already exist. But, with the increased longevity of citizens in modern advanced nations, the need for such services is bound to increase considerably in the course of the present century. And, this is something to be thankful for. The scare campaigns are no cause for alarm. On the contrary, caring for old people in their own homes will inevitably become one of our chief sources of employment, income, and consequently government revenue.

The neglect of social goods in the neoliberal era has also created major problems in mental health and drug and betting addictions. It is therefore necessary that the welfare state of the 21st century should aim to establish mental health treatment and rehabilitation centres in the suburbs and towns of the country. And, it is important that these centres should be accessible, and that privacy should be observed as much as possible. They might, for example, be established as annexes to existing health care centres staffed by frontline GPs.

A further area of neglect of social goods is the whole range of public recreation facilities, including parks, beaches, ovals, swimming pools, jetties, look-outs, gardens, town squares and other public places. Successive neoliberal governments, which have been busily trying to reconstruct our society as a perfect market, have tried, but often with not much success, to privatise these services, and to maintain these precious areas with hopelessly inadequate public funding.

Finally, I think that a new welfare state should consider establishing some 'signature industries', along the lines suggested in the final chapter of Ellis (2015). Australian manufacturers sometimes fail because they are unable to compete on global markets.

But Toyota, General Motors and Ford did not fail in Australia for this reason. They are all giants of the global car industry. They failed here only because (a) they were made to compete with each other for a share of our tiny local market, (b) they were given no adequate incentives to research and develop their products here for world markets, (c) they were required to pay their employees award wages, which are not determined at the rates required for the international markets, but at those required for local manufacturers competing with each other in the local market. Obviously, distinguished multinational firms need to be treated better than that if they are to remain in Australia to produce goods for world markets. We should, therefore, have been working with them to research and develop the car industry in Australia, and rewarding them for the service they provide for us in doing so. Chifley's original agreement with General Motors to manufacture the Holden in Australia was at least as much in our own interest, as it was in General Motors', just as any future signature industry agreement would have to be.

13

How is it all to be Paid For?

I have not asked, and do not intend to try, to answer this question. It is the job of a political philosopher to ask the right questions, as Tony Judt so strongly urged upon us. And I think that this is what I have been trying to do here. It is not my job to say what should be included in a welfare state for the 21ˢᵗ century, or how it should be paid for. It is the job of political philosophers to try to answer the basic questions concerning what we should be aiming to do. It is the job of economists to keep an eye on costs, and advise governments on how best to do what they want to do, given their objectives. Then, it is the job of politicians, who, having fixed upon their overall agenda, to determine their priorities, develop practical policies, determine what the pace of change should be, and put their programme to the electorate for endorsement.

Economists have to be relegated to the footnotes, where they belong. In the thirty or so years since the neoliberal era began, nineteenth century economic rationalists have been allowed to set the political agenda in Australia, and have been given centre stage in the political debate. But this is fundamentally wrong. The questions we should be asking are: What do we want to achieve? What is achievable? What are our priorities? How should we go about trying to implement the policies we think are best? Clearly, we shall need economic advice in trying to answer these questions. And, we should be seeking the best economic advice that we can get from academic economists. But I do not advocate populism. Our trusted advisors must be intelligent people like Joseph Stiglitz or Paul Krugman, who understand the price of inequality, and the dangers of capitalism in the 21st century. That is, they must be new economists of the 21st century, not old ones still hankering after the 'certainties' of the early 20th century.

In this essay, I have argued that Australia needs to have genuinely full employment, so that everyone who wants to be in the workforce is able to find as much work as they need. And, given this level of participation, full employment should still be no more than about 3%, as it was in the welfare state era after the war. The fact that the workforce of today is prospectively very much bigger than it was then, should make no difference to the employability of people. It should, ideally, just give them more choice in their lives. If a man or a woman wanted to take time off to pursue some other life ambition, such as to sail around the world, care for a young family, or obtain a university education, then with full employment, they should have much more opportunity to do so. For, with full employment, the only people who might remain unemployed, despite their best efforts to find work, would be those who are looking for their first job, are between jobs, are workers who lack adequate skills for the jobs on offer, or whose specific skills are not in high demand. Either that, or they must be people who live in areas where the demand for work is especially low.

But, to achieve this level of employment, we would clearly have to abandon the neoliberal social structure, and work towards the creation of a state with a strong service economy. For, if we cannot become world leaders in any one branch of technology, this is the only sustainable kind of state within which everyone can be as fully employed as they want to be. And, if we can become world leaders in some branch of technology, then so much the better. It is certainly worth a try. But our status a prosperous and happily employed nation should not be seen as depending on it.

Notes

[1] In his contribution Australia to British Empire History, edited by Sir Reginald Coupland, R. M. Crawford (1952) argued that 'Australian political life has developed a strong and resilient tradition of practical but experimental compromise. … Fundamentally it has consisted in a readiness to experiment by adaptation to circumstances rather than by the wholesale imposition of doctrinaire systems.' (pp. 190–1)

[2] This form of utilitarianism is not familiar to most philosophers, who, most commonly, distinguish only between 'act' and 'rule' utilitarianism. But the Benthamite thesis is neither of these. It is, for reasons explained fully in Ellis, 2012, a form of social contractual utilitarianism.

[3] Or, words to that effect. See Hogan 2008, Faulkner 2008, and Kirby 2008.

[4] The drafting committee was chaired by Eleanor Roosevelt, and it is likely that this moral approach to the drafting process was also hers.

[5] The 1951 Convention relating to the Status of Refugees, and the ensuing 1967 Protocol, are two such documents.

[6] There were, indeed, eight different stages in the development of the Accord over the years they were in office.

[7] The development of this movement in Britain, and its subsequent decline, were brilliantly documented in a 2013 video-documentary by Ken Loach entitled: 'The Spirit of '45'.

[8] But see my comments on pp. 54–5, for an explanation of my somewhat qualified support for globalization.

[9] In those days, health and level of education were both heavily dependent on capital.

[10] Later (in §5 below), it will be argued that morally, economically, and socially, this group of countries has in fact been in decline since the neoliberal era began, despite appearances to the contrary.

[11] In 1974, in Whitlam's time, there was in fact a current account

surplus. But, after 1980, the current account deficit began to increase, accelerated rapidly in the Howard years, and by 2008–9, it had blown out to an astonishing $20 billion for a single quarter. Most of this was household debt, i.e. not money raised for public works or corporate investment, but for spending by individuals (mostly on housing). This year (2014), our external debt stood at $1,612,746,000,000 i.e. ≈ $1.6 trillion.

[12] This was John Howard's legacy to the Australian people. The huge increase in debt financing occurred in the Howard years. Therefore, the present government's claim that this is 'Labor's debt' is simply a lie.

[13] Chifley's earlier universal public health system, modelled on the British National Health Service, was successfully opposed by the BMA (which was a precursor to the AMA) in the High Court as unconstitutional.

[14] Which was higher than at any time since the Great Depression.

[15] Australians could not live with dignity in Australia, as Australian citizens, on the wages that the workers in India or China are paid. And, it would be quite unrealistic to expect them to do so.

[16] who is Scheuer Family Professor of Philosophy Emeritus at Swarthmore College, USA, and an Adjunct Professor of the Institute of Advanced Studies at the University of Sao Paulo, Brazil,

[17] I am told that he survived only on Communist preferences.

[18] FlagPost: Women in the Australian Workforce: A 2013 Update. Parliament of Australia.

[19] In my view, mathematics, science and technology have always been the principal drivers of wealth creation. But this thesis is more controversial. Spence (2011), for example, thinks that the principal drivers of wealth creation since the 18th century were the entrepreneurs of the capitalist world. But for a contrary opinion see Ellis (2015, §6.2).

References

Bell, S. (1997): *Ungoverning the Economy*. Melbourne; Oxford University Press.

Cogwill, M. (2013): *A Shrinking Slice of the Pie*. ACTU; Working Australia Paper, No. 1

Collins, H. (1985): 'Political Ideology in Australia: The Distinctiveness of a Benthamite Society', in S. Graubard (ed.) *Australia: The Daedalus Symposium*, (published in 1985 as an issue of Daedalus). Melbourne: Angus and Robertson.

Crawford, R. M. (1952): *Australia*. London; Hutchinson's University Library.

Ellis, B. D. (2012): *Social Humanism: A New Metaphysics*. New York and London; Routledge.

Ellis, B. D. (2015): *Rationalism: In Science and Social Theory*. Melbourne; Australian Scholarly Publishing.

Faulkner, J. (2008): 'In the Tradition of Pragmatic Idealism.' Speech to launch Ashley Hogan's book, Edgecliff Sydney. <http://evatt/org.au/papers>

Fraser, M., with Roberts, C. (2014): *Dangerous Allies*. Melbourne; Melbourne University Press.

Gleeson-White, J. (2014): *Six Capitals: The Revolution Capitalism has to have—or Can Accountants Save the Planet?* London; Allen and Unwin.

Helévy, E. (1972): *The Growth of Philosophic Radicalism*. London; Faber and Faber.

Hogan, A. (2008): *Moving in the Open Daylight*; Doc Evatt, an Australian at the United Nations. Sydney; Sydney University Press.

Judt, T. (2010): *Ill Fares the Land*. London; Allen Lane.

Kirby, M (2008): 'H. V. Evatt and the United Nations; After 60 Years.'

H. V. Evatt Lecture 2008.

Kline, N. (2014): *This Changes Everything: Capitalism vs Climate*. London; Allen Lane.

Lynch, A. (forthcoming): 'The Contemporary Development Paradigm: Towards a Critical Understanding of Neoliberal Agency'. Unpublished manuscript. (Copies available for teaching purposes only.)

Metin, A. (1901/1977): *Socialisme sans doctrines*, F. Alcan, translated by Russel Ward as Socialism without Doctrine. Chippendale, NSW; Alternative Publishing Cooperative.

Meyer, T., with Hinchman, L. (2007): *The Theory of Social Democracy*. Cambridge UK and Maiden MA; Polity Press. Translated from the German Theorie der sozialen Democratie (2005)

Nozick, R. (1974): *Anarchy, State and Utopia*, Oxford; Basil Blackwell.

Rawls, J. (1971): *A Theory of Justice*. London; Oxford University Press.

Rosanvallon, P., with Goldhammer, A. (2013): *The Society of Equals*. Translated from the French Société des égaux (2011). Cambridge, Mass.; Harvard University Press.

Sen, A. (1993): 'Capability and Well-being', in M. Nussbaum and A. Sen eds. *The Quality of Life*, pp. 30–53.

Spence, A. M. (2011). *The Next Convergence: The Future of Economic Growth in a Multispeed World*. New York: Farrar, Straus and Giroux.

Stiglitz, J. (2012): *The Price of Inequality*. Allan Lane

Walras, L. (1900/1977): *Elements of Pure Economics, or The Theory of Social Wealth*, translated by William Jaffe. Fairfield; Augustus M. Kelley, Publishers.

Internet references

1. Australia's Private Debt

http://www.smh.com.au/business/the-economy/australian-households-awash-with-debt-barclays-20150316-1lzyz4.html

2. Unemployment in Australia

Google: <Australian Unemployment Rate Graph Images>

Printed in Australia
AUOC02n0809070316
274295AU00003B/3/P